OXFORD BOOKWORMS LIBRARY

Factfiles

The Olympic Games

ALEX RAYNHAM

Stage 2 (700 headwords)

Series Editor: Rachel Bladon
Founder Factfiles Editor: Christine Lindop

OXFORD
UNIVERSITY PRESS

Great Clarendon Street, Oxford, OX2 6DP, United Kingdom

Oxford University Press is a department of the University of Oxford.
It furthers the University's objective of excellence in research, scholarship,
and education by publishing worldwide. Oxford is a registered trade
mark of Oxford University Press in the UK and in certain other countries

ISBN: 978 0 19 420957 1   Book
ISBN: 978 0 19 462084 0   Book and audio pack

Printed in China

Word count (main text): 6,448 words

For more information on the Oxford Bookworms Library,
visit www.oup.com/elt/gradedreaders

ACKNOWLEDGEMENTS

The publisher would like to thank the following for permission to reproduce photographs: Alamy Images pp.5 (Olympic winner, Ancient Greece/North Wind Picture Archives), 10 (1896 Athens Olympics/Interfoto), 11 (London 2012 Olympic medals/Action Plus Sports Images), 13 (London Olympic Stadium/Athol Pictures), 56 (Olympic gold medal/Jack Sullivan), 56 (Olympic flag/AKP Photos), 56 (empty gym/colinspics), 56 (National Stadium, Tokyo, Japan/JTB Media Creation, Inc.); Corbis pp.16 (London 2012 - Closing Ceremonies/Christopher Morris), 27 (Sonja Henie Skating at St. Moritz/Underwood & Underwood), 35 (2014 Sochi Paralympic Winter Games, visually impaired skiing), 44 (Japan national team training camp/Daiju Kitamura/AFLO/Nippon News); Getty Images ppiv (Olympics race/Ian Walton), 2 (Usain Bolt crossing finish line/Ian Walton), 8 (organisers of the Athens Olympics, 1906/Print Collector), 9 (100 metre race, 1896 Olympic Games/Heritage Images), 12 (Olympics cycling/Mike Powell), 13 (London Olympic Park building site/Cate Gillon), 15 (2008 Beijing Olympics opening ceremony/AFP), 17 (Olympics medal ceremony/Clive Rose), 20 (Greg Rutherford doing long jump/Adrian Dennis), 20 (pole vault/Camera 4 Fotoagentur/Ulstein Bild), 20 (Carl Lewis, 1984 Olympics/Focus On Sport), 21 (Michael Phelps, Olympics 2004/The Sydney Morning Herald), 22 (weightlifting/Dimitri Messinis), 22 (Olympics wrestling/Straffon Images/Con), 23 (boxing, 1960 Olympics/Jerry Cooke), 23 (Nadia Comaneci, gymnastics/Keystone-France), 24 (Olympics beach volleyball/Peter Parks), 24 (men's triathlon, London 2012 Olympic Games/Professional Sport), 25 (Abebe Bikila running barefoot, 1960 Olympics marathon/Central Press/Stringer), 26 (ice hockey, 1924 Olympic Games/Topical Press Agency), 29 (2014 Olympics snowboarding/ Javier Soriano), 30 (ski jumping/Frank Peters), 31 (Jamaican bobsleigh, 1988 Winter Olympics/Manny Millan), 32 (Olympics archery/Ezra Shaw), 34 (2012 London Paralympics wheelchair race/Helene Wiesenhaan), 37 (2012 London Paralympics race/Michael Steele), 39 (Men's 100 metres final, Seoul Olympics/Chris Smith/Popperfoto), 40 (Ben Johnson/Erin Combs), 43 (Youth Olympics/Adam Pretty), 45 (Youth Olympics athletics/Mark Dadswell), 46 (Cathy Freeman with Olympic torch/*The Sydney Morning Herald*), 47 (men's marathon bronze medal winner/ Roberto Schmidt), 48 (Olympic Games 1932/Ullstein Bild), 49 (sport logos/Yasuyoshi Chiba), 50 (Tokyo 2020 placards/Yoshikazu Tsuno), 51 (Nathan Douglas coaching teen/John Gichigi), 56 (runners on track/ Pete Saloutos); Mary Evans Picture Library p.6 (Greece, Olympia); Press Association Images pp.19 (Athletics - Helsinki Olympic Games 1952 - Womens Javelin/Lehtikuva/STT-Lehtikuva), 33 (Basketball - 1960 Rome Paralympic Games - USA v Israel/Tophams/Topham Picturepoint), 38 (Paralympics blind swimming/Katsumi Kasahara/AP), 42 (street sign to Jesse Owens Allee outside Berlin's Olympic Stadium/Mike Egerton/EMPICS Sport); Rex Features pp.18 (2012 London Olympic Games, Closing Ceremony), 26 (poster for the 1924 Winter Olympic Games/Colorsport), 28 (Sochi 2014 Winter Olympic Games/Wang Lili), 29 (Olympics skiing/Framck Faugere), 29 (slalom skiing, 2014 Winter Olympics/APA- PictureDesk GmbH), 31 (*Cool Runnings* film poster/ BuenaVist/Everett), 36 (Beijing 2008 Paralympic Games/Sipa Press), 42 (Jesse Owens setting the 200 metre Olympic record at the Olympics in Berlin, Germany - 1936/CSU Archives/Everett Collection); Shutterstock p.56 (swimming pool/Andresr); The Art Archive pp.4 (Olympic Games in ancient times/Kharbine-Tapabor), 4 (Ancient Greeks race chariots at Olympia/H.M. Herget/NGS Image Collection).

CONTENTS

Men's 100 metres final
London 2012 Olympics

1 Ten seconds

On a summer evening in 2012, eight men took their places at the start of a race in the London Olympic Stadium. It was the 100 metres final, and these men were some of the best, fastest, and most famous athletes in the world. There were runners from Trinidad and Tobago, the USA, Jamaica, and the Netherlands.

Around the world, about two billion people were watching the race on TV. There were about 80,000 people in the stadium that night, and the noise of the crowd was amazing. But the athletes were not thinking about the crowd. They were only thinking about the next ten seconds: ten seconds to win or lose the race; ten seconds to win a gold medal for their country.

Suddenly, it went very quiet in the stadium. Then the athletes heard the start gun, and began to run. Two seconds later, they were moving at 30 kilometres per hour. Justin Gatlin from the USA started very fast, and Yohan Blake and Tyson Gay began well, too. The famous Jamaican runner Usain Bolt was behind them at first, but soon he came nearer and nearer. Halfway through the race, Bolt was going past everybody. He was the tallest of the athletes, and with his long legs, he was soon moving away from the other runners. He finished the race in 9.63 seconds – setting a new Olympic record! Back home in Jamaica, family and friends jumped to their feet, shouting and crying excitedly.

Only the best athletes can ever compete for their country at the Olympics. Most of the athletes finished that August 2012 race in under ten seconds, but they only got to the Olympic final after thousands of hours of hard work.

The Olympics are one of the biggest competitions in world sport. There have been many Olympic Games, and many great athletes have competed in them. But how did the Games start, and when did people begin to come together for these competitions? If we want to understand the story of the Olympics, then we need to go all the way back in time to Ancient Greece...

2 The Ancient Olympics

About 2,800 years ago in Olympia, Ancient Greece, there was a race in a field near the river Alpheus. The athletes ran about 200 metres, and a man called Coroebus, from the Greek city of Elis, won. A crowd of 40,000 people shouted his name and gave him flowers. Coroebus was one of the first Olympic champions.

There are many stories about how the Olympic Games started, and we do not know which ones are true. But we know that the Ancient Greeks loved sport and went to many sports competitions. In or before 776 BCE, the Olympic Games began at Olympia, and happened every four years after that.

They were the biggest and most important of all the Greek competitions, and the kings of Ancient Greece went to Olympia to watch them. The athletes came from many cities in modern Greece, Italy, Turkey, and Africa, and later from cities in Armenia, Egypt, and Spain. At that time, there were many wars in Greece, but because athletes needed to travel to Olympia for the Games, everyone stopped fighting for a month before they started.

The earliest Olympic Games were only one day long, and were built around ceremonies for Zeus – the most important Greek god. There was only one sports event – a race of about 200 metres called the *stade*.

Discus-throwing at the Ancient Olympics

Later, the Olympic Games were three, and then five, days long. There were new races, like the *diaulos* (about 400 metres) and the *dolichos* (1,400 metres or more). By 648 BCE, you could watch fighting, horse- and chariot-racing, jumping, and throwing events at the Games. There was even a shouting event – the winner was the person with the loudest voice!

Chariot-racing

Perhaps the most difficult ancient Olympic sport was the *pankration*. *Pankration* athletes had to be very strong. They could not use their teeth or put their fingers in someone's eyes, but they could fight with their hands and feet, and in any other way. Because of this, the *pankration* was very dangerous, and athletes sometimes died in these fights.

At these early Olympics, winning athletes were given olive branches, and champions wore these on their heads at the winners' ceremony. Ancient Olympic champions did not win medals, like today's winners, but they often became famous in their home cities, and people gave them presents like money or houses. One of the greatest ancient champions was Leonidas of Rhodes. He won all the foot races at four Olympic Games!

An Ancient Olympic champion

Only men could compete at the Ancient Olympics, and married women could not even watch the Games. But every four years, a different competition took place at Olympia for young women. These games were called the Herean Games, and they began at about the same time as the Olympics. There were races and other events, and the winners became as famous as the men's champions.

The first Olympic stadium was built in the middle of the sixth century BCE, and later there were other buildings, too. The fields of Olympia slowly became a small city. There were stadiums, and also a swimming pool and a gym, and athletes used these when they were training. Most athletes and visitors to the Games slept in the fields around Olympia, but the rich people stayed in a hotel called the Leonidaion. At the centre of Olympia there was also a big building for the god Zeus. On the first day of each Olympics, people lit a flame there and it burned until the end of the Games.

By the second century BCE, Roman soldiers were taking many countries around the Mediterranean – and in 146 BCE, Greece too became a Roman country. After that, athletes began to come to the Games from all over the Roman world. The Romans built new buildings at Olympia, and they changed the Olympic Games a lot, too. Olympic sports became more bloody during these times, and athletes often died in fighting events.

The ancient Olympics went on for nearly 1,200 years. But in 393 CE, Emperor Theodosius, the king of the Romans at that time, stopped the Games because he did not want to celebrate Zeus. Over the years, the buildings at Olympia began to fall down, and people forgot about the city. But they remembered how all wars stopped during the Olympics, and how everybody – the strongest and the best, the richest and the poorest – raced and competed together in front of the crowds.

Olympia, Ancient Greece

3   A new start

In 1889, nearly 3,000 years after the first Olympic Games, a French thinker and writer called Pierre de Coubertin learned about Ancient Olympia, and had a great idea. Coubertin wanted young people to play more sport – so he decided to organize a modern 'Olympic Games'. Many of the people that Coubertin spoke to about his idea were not interested in it, but at last he found others who wanted to help him.

So in 1894, the International Olympic Committee (IOC) started. The IOC organized the first modern Games in Athens, in 1896, with forty-three different events over ten days. They decided to rebuild the 2000-year-

Pierre de Coubertin and the IOC

old Panatheniac Stadium as the centre for the modern Olympic Games. Important games took place here during Ancient Greek times – and hundreds of builders now worked to get it ready for the 1896 Olympics.

Today, thousands of athletes from all over the world compete at the Olympics. But at the first modern Games, in 1896, there were only 241 athletes from fourteen countries – and all of them were men. King George I of Greece opened the Games, and the first event was the triple jump – athletes had to jump on one foot, move onto the other foot, and then jump as far as they could. An American called James Connolly won the triple jump and became the first Olympic champion for 1,500 years! The winners of all forty-three events got silver medals and, like the ancient athletes, they also wore olive branches on their heads.

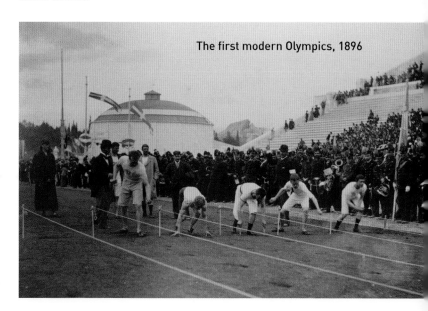

The first modern Olympics, 1896

Coubertin wanted to finish these first modern Games with a special Greek event. He remembered the famous story of a Greek soldier called Pheidippides, who, after the Greeks won an important fight against the Persians at Marathon in 490 BCE, ran 40 kilometres to bring the news to the people of Athens. So for the last event of the 1896 Games there was a 40-kilometre race from Marathon to Athens to celebrate Pheidippides' journey, and Coubertin called this 'the marathon'. When a Greek runner, Spyridon Louis, ran into the Panatheniac Stadium at the end of the marathon and won, about 100,000 people stood and shouted for him. Spyridon Louis was a poor man who usually sold water on the streets of Athens, but that day he met the king of Greece!

Spyridon Louis winning the 1896 marathon

The IOC wanted these modern Olympics to take place every four years, like the ancient Olympics, so the second modern Games were in 1900. For these, France was the host country – all the events took place there, in Paris. The Paris Olympics were five months long, and there were some very strange events – in one swimming race, the athletes had to get out of the water and climb over boats! The third modern Games were in 1904 in St Louis, USA, and for the first time, the athletes who came first, second, and third won gold, silver, and bronze medals.

silver   gold   bronze

The St Louis Olympics took place over more than four months, while another event called the World's Fair was happening in the city, and they were not very big or important. But the Games soon became shorter, bigger, and much better. Since the 1932 Los Angeles Olympics, all Olympic Games have been about two weeks long. There were other changes in the 1930s, too. After 1932, countries began to build bigger stadiums and 'Olympic villages' with rooms for all the athletes, and in 1936, the Olympics were on television for the first time!

Things have changed a lot since the first modern Games in Athens. Women could not compete in 1896, but today there are women athletes in most events, and in 2012, for the first time, every country at the Olympics had women in their team. There are also now Winter Olympic Games, and Paralympic Games for people with disabilities.

One of the most important ideas behind the Olympics is that sport is for everybody. There are hundreds of exciting events, and millions of people watch them on TV. The Olympics have become the most amazing two weeks in world sport!

Cycling
2012 London Olympics

4 The Olympics today

Before the 2012 London Olympics, Stratford in east London was not a very interesting place, and had lots of dirty old factories and buildings. The British decided to change Stratford into an amazing new centre for the Games. Thousands of people worked for many years to build a big Olympic stadium and places for swimming, cycling, and other sports.

The 2012 London Olympic stadium

Stratford, east London, before 2012

An Olympic village was built, too, with 16,000 beds for athletes and trainers. It had cinemas, gyms, a swimming pool, and places to meet friends and eat. At the Olympic village restaurant, 5,000 people could eat lunch at the same time! The 2012 Olympics cost Britain about $14 billion, but the Games were great for the country. Millions of people bought tickets for the many different events, and millions more came to Britain after the Games because they saw the country on TV and wanted to visit it.

The Olympics start in the same way every four years. In the months before each Games, Greek athletes light the Olympic torch in Ancient Olympia, and then people from the host country take the torch across the world, and

2008 Beijing Olympics opening ceremony

all around their country, before it arrives at the Olympic stadium for the opening ceremony. In the four months before the 2014 Sochi Winter Olympics, 14,000 athletes carried the Olympic torch for thousands of kilometres. It went to the Arctic, up the highest mountain in Europe, and under the water in the deepest lake in the world!

Each Olympic Games begins with an opening ceremony, and the four-hour opening ceremony for the 2008 Beijing Games was one of the best in Olympic history. The ceremony began on 08/08/2008 at 08:08:08 – because '8' is a special number in China. It started with music and some amazing dancing: people flew and danced high above the crowds!

National teams at the opening ceremony, 2012 London Olympics

Some of the things that take place in the opening ceremony are the same at every Games. Athletes from each country always walk into the stadium behind their national flags. Greece comes first, and then the other countries' teams follow. The athletes from the host country come into the stadium last. Then the host country 'opens' the Games, their national song plays, and athletes fly the Olympic flag. After that, one athlete has to make a promise: they say that they, and everyone at the Games, will compete well and not cheat.

At last, at the end of its long journey around the world, athletes bring the Olympic torch into the stadium. They use the torch to light an Olympic flame, which burns until the end of the Games – just like the flame that burned for Zeus thousands of years before.

There is a medal ceremony for the winners after each event at the Summer Olympics. The winners of silver and bronze stand on both sides of the Olympic champion, and a person from the IOC gives each athlete their medal, and flowers. Then everyone listens to the Olympic champion's national song, and the flags of all three countries fly in the stadium.

A medal ceremony

A big ceremony ends the Olympic Games. At the closing ceremony for the 2012 Olympics, people gave performances on amazing sculptures of famous London buildings inside the Olympic stadium, and the crowd listened to British singers. They also watched dancers from Brazil, because Rio de Janeiro was the host city of the next Summer Olympics. The athletes danced together and celebrated – it was an amazing party to end a great Olympic Games!

2012 London Olympics closing ceremony

5 Sports and champions

On each day of the Games, different events take place all over the Olympic city, and in other places in the host country, too. Some events, like the marathon, only take a few hours, because everyone competes at the same time. But sports like football and basketball take many days because there are lots of games. The best athletes and teams then go on to compete in the final.

All track and field events (running, jumping, and throwing) take place in the stadium – often at the same time. One afternoon at the 1952 Helsinki Olympics, the Czech athlete Emil Zátopek was running in the men's 5,000 metres while his wife, Dana Zátopková, was competing in the javelin. It was a great day for them, because they both won gold medals!

Dana Zátopková
Javelin

Long jump

Pole vault

There are lots of exciting track and field events. The best men's long jumpers can jump more than 8 metres, and in the women's javelin, athletes can throw the javelin more than 70 metres! The pole vault is another exciting sport: athletes can jump more than 5 metres high.

There have been many great Olympic sprinters – like Irena Szewińska, who won six medals for Poland in running races. But one of the most famous sprinters of all is American Carl Lewis. In four Olympic Games, between 1984 and 1996, Lewis won nine gold medals and one silver in athletics events. And he was not just a great sprinter: four of those medals were for the long jump! Carl Lewis's running races were very exciting to watch because he usually came from behind and won the race in the last 20 metres.

Carl Lewis
Sprinting

Michael Phelps
Swimming

Some of the best races at the Olympics take place in the swimming pool. At the Beijing Olympics, swimmers set twenty-five new world records, and the crowd saw some of the most exciting swimming races in Olympic history. American Michael Phelps, who is possibly the best Olympic swimmer of all time, won eight gold medals in Beijing! Phelps competed at his first Olympics in Sydney, in 2000, when he was only fifteen years old. Then, at the next three Olympic Games, he won an amazing eighteen gold medals.

But not all Olympic swimming stars are medal winners: Eric Moussambani from Equatorial Guinea became famous because he only learned to swim eight months before the Sydney Olympics. He did not get into the final for his event, and he swam his race very slowly. But when he finished, everyone in the crowd was shouting for him!

Sports events like wrestling, weightlifting, boxing, and gymnastics happen in different buildings around the Olympic city. Weightlifting is amazing to watch. The weightlifters have to hold very big heavy metal plates (weights), but the weightlifters are often very small. Turkish-Bulgarian Naim Süleymanoğlu was possibly the greatest Olympic weightlifter. He was 1.47 metres tall and weighed only 62 kilograms – but he could hold a weight of 190 kilograms!

Women's boxing only became an Olympic sport in 2012, and Britain's Nicola Adams became the first women's champion. But there have been men's boxing matches since 1904, and many great champions. The American boxing champion Cassius Clay won a gold medal at the

Women's wrestling

Naim Süleymanoğlu
Weightlifting

Rome Olympics in 1960. Later, Clay changed his name to Muhammad Ali and became very famous in America, and all around the world. When the 1996 Olympics came to Atlanta, USA, Muhammad Ali lit the Olympic flame.

Gymnastics events are always very exciting, because gymnasts can lose points for very small mistakes. They get points out of ten at their events, but in the past nobody ever got ten. Then a fourteen-year-old girl from Romania called Nadia Comăneci competed at the 1976 Montreal Olympics. She was amazing – she did nothing wrong. For the first time in Olympic history, a gymnast got ten points out of ten – and that happened seven times in Montreal!

Cassius Clay
Boxing

Nadia Comăneci
Gymnastics

Beach volleyball

Some Olympic sports happen outside, around the Olympic centre. For the Beijing Olympics beach volleyball event, the organizers made a beach in the city centre! The 2012 Olympic triathlon was in London's Hyde Park, and the swimming took place in the park's famous Serpentine Lake. The athletes had to swim 1,500 metres in the cold lake, then cycle 40 kilometres around London, and run a 10,000-metre race!

2012 London Olympics triathlon

The men's marathon is always the last athletics event of the Olympics, and thousands of people stand in the streets to watch it. There have been lots of amazing winners, and one of the greatest was the Ethiopian athlete Abebe Bikila.

Abebe Bikila got into the Ethiopian team at the last moment before the Rome Olympic Games in 1960. The team organizers gave him some running shoes, but they were too big, so he ran the Olympic marathon through the streets of Rome without any shoes. When he went to the front in the last kilometre and won the race, Bikila became the first Ethiopian Olympic champion in history. Before the race, nobody thought that Bikila was going to win, so at the medal ceremony, nobody knew how to play the national song of Ethiopia.

Six weeks before the next Olympics at Tokyo in 1964, Bikila became very ill and went into hospital. But amazingly he got better, ran in the Olympic marathon, and won it. He was the first person to win the Olympic marathon twice. This time, everyone was ready to play his national song!

Abebe Bikila, Rome marathon, 1960

6 The Winter Olympics

In 1924, 258 athletes competed in a 'Winter Sports Week' in the mountains of Chamonix, France. It was a small competition, with only a few sports, like ice hockey and figure skating. But it was the start of the Winter Olympic Games, and they took place every four years after that.

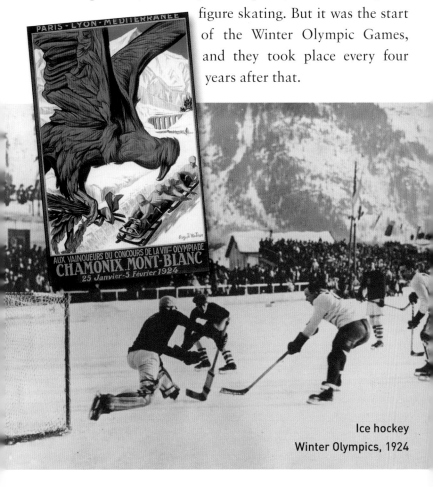

Ice hockey
Winter Olympics, 1924

Sonja Henie
Figure skating

The second Winter Olympics were in 1928 in St Moritz, Switzerland, and one of the best athletes of the Games was fifteen-year-old figure skater Sonja Henie, from Norway. After she stopped competing in ice skating events in 1936, she became a Hollywood film star!

The first few Winter Games were small, but they quickly became much bigger, with more than a thousand athletes from 1964. At the amazing 2014 Winter Olympics in Sochi, Russia, about 2,800 athletes competed. The Russians spent over $50 billion on the Games, which were the most expensive Olympics in history.

Warm weather is a big problem for the Winter Olympics because many of the sports need snow. So the winter before the Sochi Olympics, the Russians put a lot of snow in special places high in the mountains and kept it cold there all year until the Games!

Speed skating

For some Winter Olympic events, like ice hockey and speed skating, the weather is not important because they take place inside. Speed skating is very exciting to watch: it is fast and dangerous, and skaters can go at more than 50 kilometres per hour.

The Dutch speed skater Yvonne van Gennip became a champion in the 1988 Calgary Winter Olympics. She hurt her foot two months before the Games, and nobody thought that she could win when she started the 3,000 metres race. But it was the best race of Yvonne's life. She set a new world record and won a gold medal!

Christa Luding was another famous speed skater – but like some other athletes, she also competed at the Summer Olympics! In 1988, she won gold and silver medals for speed skating at the Calgary Winter Olympics in Canada, and a silver medal for cycling at the Summer Games in Seoul, South Korea.

Of course, some of the most famous competitions of the Winter Olympics are the skiing and snowboarding events. People wait for hours in the snow to watch stars like American snowboarding champion Shaun White

Skiing

Snowboarding

and Norwegian skier Marit Bjoergen. Many people also remember the great Italian skier Alberto Tomba, who won five medals at three Winter Games.

One of Tomba's best races was the slalom at the 1994 Lillehammer Winter Olympics. Slalom skiers race between flags, and they go down the mountain twice. On Tomba's second time down the mountain, he started in twelfth place. He nearly fell, but then he did better and better and raced his way to a silver medal!

Slalom skiing

Winter sports can be very dangerous. Some Winter Olympic athletes have died during races and events in the past, and other people have had very lucky escapes. At the 1998 Games in Nagano, Japan, Austrian skier Hermann Maier was racing down a mountain at 130 kilometres per hour when he suddenly hit something and his body flew up 10 metres high. When he hit the ground, people ran to him. They thought that he was dead, but then Maier stood up and walked away. He later won three Olympic medals at the Nagano Games!

Japanese athlete Masahiko Harada became famous at Nagano, too. The Japanese ski jumping team was in first place in the event, but then Harada made the worst jump of his life, which pushed his team down into fourth place. But then on his next jump, he surprised everyone. Harada jumped 137 metres, setting a new Olympic record. Thanks to Harada's amazing jump, the Japanese team won the gold medal, and Harada became famous in Japan.

Masahiko Harada
Ski jumping, 1998 Nagano Olympics

One of the most dangerous Winter Olympic sports is bobsleigh racing. Athletes race between walls of ice at 150 kilometres per hour. Most bobsleigh teams are from countries that have cold winters, but amazingly, Jamaica – which never has any snow – has a Winter Olympic bobsleigh team! In 1987, some friends in Jamaica made a bobsleigh and raced it on wheels down hills and streets. That autumn, they went down a real bobsleigh track – on ice – for the first time. The Jamaicans only had a few months to train, but they competed at the 1988 Calgary Winter Olympics! The Jamaicans did not win any medals in Calgary, but since then, they have competed in five more Winter Games. There is a film about them, and when they arrived in Sochi, all the athletes wanted to be in a photo with them!

From the film *Cool Runnings*

The Jamaican bobsleigh team, 1988 Calgary Winter Olympics

7 The Paralympics

Because he fell under a train when he was young, George Eyser only had one leg. But he still became a gymnast. In 1904, the Olympics came to his hometown – St Louis, USA – and Eyser competed in gymnastics and the triathlon. The other athletes in his events did not have disabilities, but he won six Olympic medals, and three of them were gold.

Other athletes with disabilities have also competed at the Olympic Games and won medals. Im Dong-Hyun, from Korea, is visually impaired, and he won two gold medals and one bronze for archery at the Athens, Beijing, and London Olympics. But most athletes with disabilities compete in a different Olympics called the Paralympic Games.

Im Dong-Hyun
Archery, 2008 Beijing Olympics

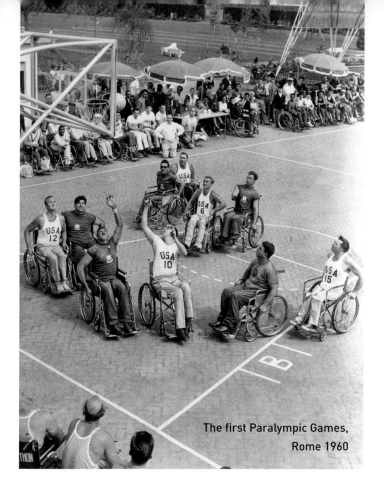

The first Paralympic Games,
Rome 1960

The idea of Olympics for athletes with disabilities first came from a man called Dr Ludwig Guttmann. He was working at Stoke Mandeville Hospital in England at the time of the 1948 London Olympics, and he decided to organize an archery competition for wheelchair users at the hospital. Everyone enjoyed the competition, so after that, the hospital had a wheelchair sports event every year. In 1952, a team from the Netherlands came to compete in the event, and after that, the competition got bigger and bigger. Then, in 1960, the IOC and Stoke Mandeville Hospital worked together to organize the first Paralympic Games in Rome.

Wheelchair racing

Four hundred athletes from twenty-one countries came to these first Paralympics, and since then, the Games have got a lot bigger. The first few Paralympics were only for wheelchair users, but visually impaired people and people who only have one arm or leg competed for the first time in 1976. The first Winter Paralympics took place that year, too, in Örnsköldsvik, Sweden. Now the Paralympic Games happen immediately after the Summer Olympics, and the Winter Paralympics after the Winter Games – and in the same cities, too. More than 4,000 athletes from 160 countries will compete at the 2016 Rio de Janeiro Paralympics.

There are different Paralympic events for athletes with different disabilities, and there are different events for people with the same disability, too. For example, there are races for visually impaired people who can only see a little, and different races for athletes who are blind – who cannot see at all.

When they watch races for visually impaired people, the crowd in the Olympic stadium have to stay quiet, because the runners need to hear well. People who can see run next to the athletes on the track, and the athletes listen to their voices to find their way. Visually impaired athletes in swimming races have help, too, from people who stand next to the swimming pool and make a noise or touch the swimmer's bodies when they need to turn.

The most dangerous Paralympic events are in the Winter Paralympics. When visually impaired skiers race, other people ski with them, talking to them by radio while they go down the mountain at over 100 kilometres per hour!

Visually impaired skiing

One of the oldest Paralympic sports is wheelchair basketball, and the matches are fast and exciting. An athlete's Paralympic wheelchair is built specially for their body, and is very fast. An athlete can move at more than 30 kilometres per hour in a wheelchair, and can turn very quickly.

Wheelchair basketball

Running on blades

blade

Very big crowds watch wheelchair basketball. But many people's favourite Paralympic events are the races for runners on blades. Athletes on blades can go as fast as Olympic sprinters, and they often train with runners who do not have disabilities.

There are many disabled athletes who have done amazing things, like Italian Roberto Marson, who, between 1964 and 1976, won twenty-six Paralympic medals in different sports. But perhaps the most famous Paralympic athlete of all time was the American Trischa Zorn.

Trischa Zorn was born blind, but she began to swim when she was seven years old. She became the best swimmer in Paralympic history, and for a long time, nobody could swim faster than her. At the 1988 Paralympics in Seoul, Korea, Zorn won gold medals in all of her ten events! Before she stopped competing, she swam in seven Paralympic Games. She won an amazing fifty-five Paralympic medals, and forty-one of those medals were gold!

Trischa Zorn

8 Problems at the Olympics

Eight athletes ran in the final of the men's 100 metres at the 1988 Seoul Olympics. But most of the 90,000 people in the stadium that day were only watching two men: Canadian Ben Johnson and American Carl Lewis. They were the most famous sprinters in the world. Their faces were in the newspapers and on TV all the time. While the runners got ready, people around the world watched and waited. Who was the best?

Men's 100 metres final, Seoul 1988 Olympics

When Ben Johnson finished first, people all over Canada celebrated. But forty-eight hours later, the IOC said that there were steroids in Ben Johnson's blood, and took away his medal. People can run faster when they take steroids, so this is cheating. Olympic doctors take blood from athletes at each Olympic Games, and if they find steroids in the athlete's blood, the IOC stops them from competing.

Ben Johnson after the IOC took away his medal

Most Olympic athletes compete well, but there have always been some people who try to cheat. After the 2000 Sydney Paralympics, the winning wheelchair basketball team had to give back their medals because some of the athletes did not have disabilities. Perhaps the Olympics' funniest cheat was American Fred Lorz, who competed in the 1904 St Louis marathon – he travelled 17 kilometres in a car!

But cheating is not the only problem in the long history of the Olympics. There was nearly a terrible day at the Atlanta Olympics in 1996, when an American man put a bomb in a park which was at the centre of the Atlanta Games. There were very big crowds in the park at the time. But luckily, a man called Richard Jewell found the bomb and told people to run away. One person still died, but Jewell's quick thinking stopped that day from becoming one of the worst in Olympic history.

In Ancient Greece, all fighting and wars stopped for the Olympics, but this has not happened in modern times. In 1916, 1940, and 1944, there were no Olympic Games because of the First and Second World Wars.

Wars have darkened the Olympics at other times, too, but one of the greatest Olympic stories comes from the 1936 Olympic Games, which were opened by Adolf Hitler in Berlin. Hitler was a racist – he thought that white Germans were the world's best people, and the world's best athletes, and he thought that other people were no good.

At the Berlin Olympics, Hitler wanted white Germans to win many of the events. He wanted the world to think that his ideas were right. But the star of that Games was

Jesse Owens, 1936 Berlin Olympics

a black American sprinter and long jumper called Jesse Owens. Jesse Owens won four gold medals in Berlin, and many people who watched his races and jumps knew that Hitler's racist ideas were stupid and wrong. People have not forgotten Jesse Owens: today, near the old Olympic stadium in Berlin, you can walk down Jesse Owens Street.

Jesse Owens Street, Berlin

9 Becoming an Olympic hero

Every athlete has a long, hard journey to get to the Olympics. Around the world, thousands of young sportspeople train six days a week for many hours each day for years and years, because they want to become an Olympic hero.

Some famous Olympic athletes began training in their sports when they were as young as eight. Time is a big problem for many young athletes because it is difficult for them to do school work when they are training every evening. Their families often have to spend a lot of money to help them, and they have to give a lot of their time, too. And sometimes they have to move to another city – because the young athlete needs better training.

Young athletes BMX racing

Ajinomoto National Training Center

Many countries have big training centres for young athletes. There are hundreds of young Japanese athletes at the Ajinomoto National Training Center in Kita, Tokyo. The centre has swimming pools and gyms, and places for many other sports. Doctors and trainers at the centre work together with people who watch how athletes use their bodies and then plan meals for them. Computers look at how well the athletes do, to help them learn from their mistakes and train better. The centre is an amazing place, and it has helped thousands of young athletes.

It is important for young athletes to compete a lot, and to do well in national and international sports competitions. When they get older and better, they begin to travel more and more. They compete all around the world and train for other important international competitions like the Commonwealth Games, the IAAF World Championships, and the Youth Olympic Games.

In 2010, 204 countries sent teams to Singapore for the first ever Youth Olympic Games. Then, in 2012, the first Winter Youth Olympics took place in Innsbruck, Austria. Athletes at the Youth Olympics are fourteen to eighteen years old, and many of them later compete for their country at the Olympic Games.

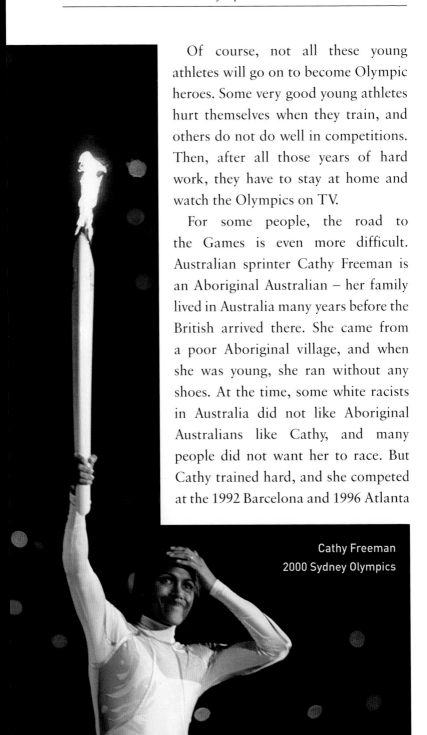

Of course, not all these young athletes will go on to become Olympic heroes. Some very good young athletes hurt themselves when they train, and others do not do well in competitions. Then, after all those years of hard work, they have to stay at home and watch the Olympics on TV.

For some people, the road to the Games is even more difficult. Australian sprinter Cathy Freeman is an Aboriginal Australian – her family lived in Australia many years before the British arrived there. She came from a poor Aboriginal village, and when she was young, she ran without any shoes. At the time, some white racists in Australia did not like Aboriginal Australians like Cathy, and many people did not want her to race. But Cathy trained hard, and she competed at the 1992 Barcelona and 1996 Atlanta

Cathy Freeman
2000 Sydney Olympics

Vanderlei de Lima
2004 Athens Olympics

Games, and won a silver medal. Then, in 2000, when the Olympics came to Sydney, Australia, Cathy won a gold medal in the 400 metres. She lit the flame at the opening ceremony, too.

Athletes try very, very hard to win. But the Olympics are not only about winning. At the 2004 Athens Olympics, Brazilian Vanderlei de Lima was in first place in the marathon when a man ran out of the crowd and tried to fight with him. Two athletes went past him, but then someone helped to free de Lima, and he started running again. Everyone shouted for him when he ran into the Panatheniac Stadium and finished in third place.

The Olympics are about helping other people, too. In 1988, Canadian Lawrence Lemieux was in second place in an Olympic sailing race when he saw another boat in trouble. Lemieux lost the race because he stopped to help the people on the boat, but the IOC gave him a Pierre de Coubertin medal. This special medal is for athletes who are a great example to other people, and very few people have ever won it.

Two friends from Japan had a different kind of medal from the Olympic Games, too. At the 1936 Berlin Olympics, Shuhei Nishida and Sueo Oe competed in the pole vault. They each jumped 4.25 metres – the second best in the event. But at that time, the organizers said that they could not both win a silver medal. In the end, Oe took the bronze medal and Nishida took the silver. But when they got back to Japan, the two friends cut their medals in half and put each half together to make new ones. You can see one of these special medals in Waseda, Japan today. It is half-silver, half-bronze – and it tells us what true Olympic heroes are really like.

Shuhei Nishida
Pole vault,
1936 Berlin
Olympics

10   Into the future

In 2016, the Olympic Games will come to South America for the first time. They will take place in Rio de Janeiro – one of the most beautiful cities in the world.

Many of the events will happen at a big new Olympic Park in the west of Rio, between the mountains and the sea. The Barra da Tijuca Olympic Park will have an Olympic village with rooms for 17,000 athletes and trainers, a big Olympic training centre, and buildings for fifteen different sports.

Other events will happen all around the city, and in other places in Brazil. The track and field events will be in the João Havelange Olympic Stadium in Maracanã, Rio, and the beach volleyball matches will take place on Rio's world-famous Copacabana Beach. People will watch football matches in the great Maracanã Stadium, and also in São Paulo, Belo Horizonte, Salvador, and Brasília.

Pictures from the 2016 Rio de Janeiro Olympics

In all, Brazil will spend about $26 billion as the host country for the 2016 Olympic Games. And because Rio is the home of samba dancing and the Carnival – the biggest street party in the world – many people think that the opening ceremony of the 2016 Games will be one of the most amazing in Olympic history.

PyeongChang in South Korea is the host city for the 2018 Winter Olympics, and in 2020 the Summer Games will be in another of the world's greatest cities – Tokyo, Japan.

Each Olympic Games is exciting and different, and the events at the Olympics are changing all the time, too. We do not know what sports will be in the Olympics in fifty or one hundred years' time. But we do know that all around the world, young sportspeople will still have one hope: competing in the Olympic Games – and winning a medal for their country.

GLOSSARY

amazing *(adj)* exciting and interesting

ancient *(adj)* very old; from a time long ago

athlete *(n)* a person who is good at sports like running or jumping

become *(v)* to begin to be something (past tense **became**)

blade *(n)* a long piece of metal that athletes who have one leg or no legs wear for running

bomb *(n)* a thing that explodes, hurting people or breaking things

bronze *(adj)* a dark red-brown metal

celebrate *(v)* to do something special because you are happy or because it is an important time, e.g. a birthday

ceremony *(n)* an important time when people come to a place or building to do special things

champion *(n)* a person who is the best at a sport or game

cheat *(v & n)* to do something that is not honest or fair

city *(n)* a big and important town

compete *(v)* to try to win a race or a competition

competition *(n)* a game etc. that people try to win

disability *(n)* when you cannot use a part of your body well or easily, or cannot learn easily; **disabled** *(adj)*

event *(n)* a race or competition

final *(n & adj)* the last game or race in a competition, for the winners of the earlier games or races

flag *(n)* a piece of cloth on a stick with special colours or pictures for a country

flame *(n)* You see hot, bright flames when something is on fire.

gym *(n)* a room or building (sometimes with special machines, etc.) for doing physical exercise, e.g. sport

history *(n)* all the things that happened before now

idea *(n)* a plan, or something you think of

king *(n)* the most important man in a country

match *(n)* a game between two people or teams

medal *(n)*   a piece of metal like a big coin with words and pictures on it; you get it when you win a competition or race

national *(adj)*   from or about a country

olive branch *(n)*   a thin piece of wood from a tree which has small strong-tasting green or black fruit on it

organize *(v)*   to plan something or get it ready

point *(n)*   a mark that you win in a game or sport

problem *(n)*   something that is difficult; something that you worry about

race *(n & v)*   a competition to see who can run, drive, ride, etc. the fastest

sculpture *(n)*   a thing made from stone, wood, etc. by an artist

set a record *(v)*   to do the best, fastest, highest, lowest, etc. that has been done in a sport

sprint *(v)*   to run very fast for a short time

stadium *(n)*   a place with seats around it where you can watch sport

swimming pool *(n)*   a place for swimming

take place *(v)*   to happen (past tense **took place**)

team *(n)*   a group of people who play a sport or a game together against another group

throw *(v)*   to move your arm quickly to send something through the air (past tense **threw**)

torch *(n)*   a light that you can carry

train *(v)*   to teach a person or an animal to do something; **trainer** *(n)*

visually impaired *(adj)*   when you cannot see well

war *(n)*   fighting between countries or between groups of people

wheelchair *(n)*   a chair with wheels for somebody who cannot walk well

MODERN SUMMER OLYMPICS HOST COUNTRIES

Year	City	Country
1896	Athens	Greece
1900	Paris	France
1904	St Louis	United States
1908	London	United Kingdom
1912	Stockholm	Sweden
1920	Antwerp	Belgium
1924	Paris	France
1928	Amsterdam	Netherlands
1932	Los Angeles	United States
1936	Berlin	Germany
1948	London	United Kingdom
1952	Helsinki	Finland
1956	Melbourne	Australia
1960	Rome	Italy
1964	Tokyo	Japan
1968	Mexico City	Mexico
1972	Munich	West Germany
1976	Montreal	Canada
1980	Moscow	Soviet Union
1984	Los Angeles	United States
1988	Seoul	South Korea
1992	Barcelona	Spain
1996	Atlanta	United States
2000	Sydney	Australia
2004	Athens	Greece
2008	Beijing	China
2012	London	United Kingdom
2016	Rio de Janeiro	Brazil
2020	Tokyo	Japan

ACTIVITIES

Before reading

1 **Match the words to the pictures.**

flag, gym, medal, race, stadium, swimming pool

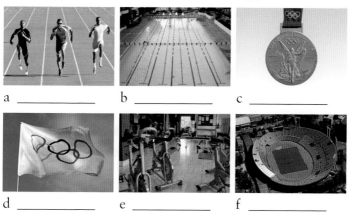

a _____   b _____   c _____

d _____   e _____   f _____

2 **How much do you know about the Olympics? Are these sentences true or false?**

1 Millions of people around the world watch the Olympic Games on TV.

2 The Games always happen in the same place.

3 The Games are nearly 3,000 years old.

4 The marathon first became an event at the Olympics more than 2,000 years ago.

5 Only the first two athletes or teams in an event get Olympic medals.

6 There is a different Olympic Games for athletes with disabilities.

ACTIVITIES

While reading

Read Chapter 1. Complete the sentences with the words below. There is one word which you do not need.

compete, final, flag, medal, noise, record

1 Eight athletes ran in the _____ of the men's 100 metres in 2012.

2 The _____ of the crowd in the stadium that night was amazing.

3 Everyone in the race wanted to win a gold _____ for their country.

4 Usain Bolt set a new Olympic _____ when he won the race in 9.63 seconds.

5 Only the best athletes can ever _____ for their country at the Olympics.

Read Chapter 2. Put the events in order.

a Greece became a Roman country.

b The buildings at Olympia began to fall down.

c Olympic sports became more bloody.

d A one-day event began at Olympia, in Greece.

e Emperor Theodosius stopped the Games.

f The Ancient Greeks built the first Olympic stadium.

Read Chapter 3. Change the <u>underlined</u> word to make the sentences true.

1 Pierre de Coubertin was a French <u>athlete</u> and thinker.
2 Winners of events at the first modern Olympics got <u>gold</u> medals.
3 Spyridon Louis won the Olympic <u>javelin</u>.
4 Today, the Olympic Games are about two <u>months</u> long.
5 No <u>men</u> competed in the first modern Olympic Games.

Read Chapter 4. Complete the sentences with numbers.

1 An Olympic village for _____ athletes and trainers was built for the 2012 Games.
2 The Games cost Britain $_____ billion.
3 _____ athletes carried the Sochi Winter Olympic torch.
4 The Beijing Olympics opening ceremony was _____ hours long.
5 _____ is a special number in China.

Read Chapter 5. Match the people to their sports.

1 Emil Zátopek   a boxing
2 Dana Zátopková   b swimming
3 Carl Lewis   c marathon
4 Michael Phelps   d javelin
5 Naim Süleymanoğlu   e gymnastics
6 Nicola Adams   f sprinting and long jump
7 Nadia Comăneci   g weightlifting
8 Abebe Bikila   h 5,000 metres

Read Chapter 6. Complete the sentences.

1 Sonja Henie was a famous Olympic _____.
2 _____ can be a big problem at the Winter Games
  because many of the sports need snow.
3 _____ can go at more than 50 kilometres per
  hour.
4 _____ skiers like Alberto Tomba race down a
  mountain between flags.
5 The Jamaican bobsleigh team is amazing because
  Jamaica does not have any _____.

Read Chapter 7. Match the sentence halves.

1 Im Dong-Hyun is visually impaired, but…
2 The first few Paralympic Games were only…
3 The Summer and Winter Paralympic Games now…
4 Today there are different events…
5 The crowds must be very quiet…
6 Wheelchair basketball is…
7 Athletes on blades often train…

a for athletes with different disabilities.
b one of the oldest Paralympic sports.
c take place immediately after the Summer and Winter
  Olympics.
d when visually impaired people race.
e he has won three Olympic medals.
f with runners who have no disabilities.
g for wheelchair users.

Read Chapter 8. Complete the sentences.

1 The IOC took away Ben Johnson's medal because he
   took _____ before the 1988 Seoul Olympics.
2 The IOC has doctors who take _____ from
   athletes at each Games.
3 In the St Louis Olympic marathon, Fred Lorz used a
   _____ to cheat.
4 Somebody left a _____ in a park at the 1996
   Atlanta Games.
5 In 1916, 1940, and 1944, _____ stopped the
   Games.

Read Chapter 9. Complete the paragraph with the words.

compete, international, move, team, train

All Olympic athletes ¹_____ very hard. Some young
athletes' families ²_____ to a different city, because
their children need better training. Young athletes have
to ³_____ in events a lot, and they need to do well
in national and ⁴_____ sports competitions. But
only the best can ever get into their country's Olympic
⁵_____.

**Read Chapter 10. Are the sentences true, false, or not
mentioned in the chapter?**

1 All events in the 2016 Olympics will be in Rio de Janeiro.
2 Samba dancing comes from Rio.
3 The 2018 Winter Olympics will be in South Korea.
4 There will be four new events at the 2020 Olympics.
5 Sportspeople will always want to win medals.

ACTIVITIES

After reading

Vocabulary

1 **Read the clues and complete the word puzzle. What is the hidden word?**

1 At the Paralympics, many athletes compete in _____ basketball.

2 A few Olympic athletes have taken steroids and tried to _____ .

3 The Olympic _____ burns in the stadium until the end of the Games.

4 There is a medal _____ after each event.

5 Nadia Comăneci was the first gymnast who got ten _____ out of ten at the Olympics.

6 Ancient Olympic champions were given _____ branches to wear on their heads.

7 Rome was the _____ city for the 1960 Olympics.

8 _____ run in short races like the 100 metres.

Grammar

1 **Choose the correct quantifiers to complete the sentences.**

1 The Olympic Games take place *every / each* four years.
2 *A few / All* athletes train very hard for their events.
3 There are *lots of / much* good athletes, so it is very hard to get into the Olympic team.
4 Young athletes do not have *much / many* free time.
5 Only *a little / a few* people can run the 100 metres in under 10 seconds.

2 **Complete the interview between an Olympic champion and a TV reporter. Use the past simple or present perfect form of the verbs in brackets.**

REPORTER: You [1]_____ (just win) the women's 1,500 metres. How do you feel?

ATHLETE: Great! I [2]_____ (run) in a lot of international competitions, but I [3]_____ (not got) an Olympic medal before.

REPORTER: Yes, you [4]_____ (be) a 1,500-metre runner for years, but you [5]_____ (not compete) in the last Games. Why [6]_____ (be) that?

ATHLETE: I [7]_____ (hurt) my leg two weeks before the last Games, so I [8]_____ (have to) sit at home and watch the race on TV. It [9]_____ (take) me a long time to start training again after that.

REPORTER: Well, you [10]_____ (work) very hard since then!

ATHLETE: Yes, I have. But I [11]_____ (not think) that I would become an Olympic champion.

Reading

1 Find people in the book to match the descriptions.

This person…
1 won the marathon in the first modern Olympic Games.
    _____ (Chapter 3)
2 became the first women's Olympic boxing champion.
    _____ (Chapter 5)
3 hurt her foot before the 1988 Winter Olympics, but set a
    world record. _____ (Chapter 6)
4 won four gold medals at the 1936 Olympics.
    _____ (Chapter 8)
5 won a special medal because he stopped racing to help
    other people. _____ (Chapter 9)

2 How much can you remember? Write the answers.

1 What ancient Games did women compete in?

    _____

2 Who decided to start the modern Olympic Games?

    _____

3 Which team goes into the Olympic stadium first at every
    opening ceremony? _____

4 Which champion boxer changed his name and became
    very famous around the world? _____

5 Where were the 2014 Winter Olympics? _____

6 Which hospital in England helped to organize the first
    Paralympics? _____

7 What is the host city for the 2020 Summer Olympics?

    _____

Writing

1 Read the news report, and answer the question.

Ben Johnson loses Olympic medal

Two days ago in Seoul, the world watched Ben Johnson when he won the race of his life – the men's 100 metres. But today the IOC have said that it is taking away his medal. After the race, it found steroids in his blood. All over Canada today, people are asking why – why do athletes cheat?

What happened to Ben Johnson after he won the 100 metres?

2 Now write a news report about the Jamaican bobsleigh team. Use these notes to help you.

- Jamaican bobsleigh team arrive in Sochi
- the crowd and other athletes want to be in photos with them
- famous all over the world
- first competed at the 1988 Calgary Olympics
- have competed in five Winter Olympics since then
- amazing because Jamaica has no snow

3 Choose one of these headlines. Write a short news report.

MAN IN CROWD TRIES TO STOP ATHENS MARATHON RUNNER

CATHY FREEMAN'S LONG ROAD TO THE OLYMPICS

Speaking

1 Read the dialogue. What two things do both speakers agree on?

MAX: I really enjoy the Olympic Games.

JESS: So do I. My favourite sports are the track and field events.

MAX: Really? I prefer gymnastics. The gymnasts do amazing things.

JESS: You're right about that. They're very good. But I like a good race more.

2 Look at the dialogue above and …

- underline three ways to agree or disagree.
- circle three ways to express preferences.

3 Imagine you are going to visit Tokyo during the 2020 Summer Olympics or Paralympics, and you can only buy tickets to three different events. Discuss the questions in pairs.

- Which Olympic events do you want to go to, and why?
- Would you prefer to go to indoor or outdoor events?
- What other things are you going to do in Tokyo? (for example, shopping, visiting places)

INDEX

THE OXFORD BOOKWORMS LIBRARY

THE OXFORD BOOKWORMS LIBRARY is a best-selling series of graded readers which provides authentic and enjoyable reading in English. It includes a wide range of original and adapted texts: classic and modern fiction, non-fiction, and plays. There are more than 250 Bookworms to choose from, in seven carefully graded language stages that go from beginner to advanced level.

Each Bookworms Factfile has full colour photographs, and offers extensive support, including:

▸ extra support pages, including a glossary of above-level words
▸ activities to develop language and communication skills
▸ a complete audio recording
▸ online tests

Each Bookworm pack contains a reader and audio.

4 STAGE 4	▸ 1400 HEADWORDS	▸ CEFR B1–B2
3 STAGE 3	▸ 1000 HEADWORDS	▸ CEFR B1
2 STAGE 2	▸ 700 HEADWORDS	▸ CEFR A2–B1
1 STAGE 1	▸ 400 HEADWORDS	▸ CEFR A1–A2

Find a full list of *Bookworms* and resources at
www.oup.com/elt/gradedreaders

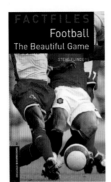

If you liked this Factfile, why not try...

Football: The Beautiful Game
STEVE FLINDERS

Some call it football, some call it soccer, and to others it's the beautiful game. By any name, it's a sport with some fascinating stories.

OXFORD BOOKWORMS LIBRARY

Audio Download

Stage 2

The Olympic Games

To download the audio for this title

1 Go to www.oup.com/elt/download

2 Use this code and your email address

Your download code

OXFORD
UNIVERSITY PRESS

ISBN 978-0-19-462190-8

9 780194 621908

The Olympic Games

Every four years, the world's best athletes come together for one of the most exciting competitions in sport: the Olympic Games. After years of training, competitors in more than forty different sports win and lose their events, and set new world records, in front of crowds of people.

The Olympic Games are more than two thousand five hundred years old. So how did they start, how have they changed over the years, and what have been some of the most important times in their history?   (Word count 6,448)

◄ STAGE 6
◄ STAGE 5
◄ STAGE 4
◄ STAGE 3
◄ STAGE 2
◄ STAGE 1
◄ STARTER

 FACTFILES

 AUDIO AVAILABLE

Cover image courtesy of Getty Images (Golden Laurel Wreath/Ulf Boettcher/LOOK-foto)

STAGE 2 700 Headwords

SHAPING learning TOGETHER

OXFORD
UNIVERSITY PRESS

www.oup.com/elt

CEFR
B1
A2
A1

ISBN 978-0-19-420957-1

9 780194 209571

New York

JOHN ESCOTT